# NO Trespassing - This Is MY Body!

By Pattie Fitzgerald

safely ever after, inc.

# NO Trespassing - This Is MY Body!
## By Pattie Fitzgerald

*For Mark and Marissa… the reason for everything*

---

Special Thanks:
Linda Perry
Dr. Jay Gordon
Danna Teal
Silvana Horn
Barbara Gervase
Jennie Pica
Vincent Pica

---

Text Copyright ©2011 by Pattie Fitzgerald    Illustrations Copyright ©2011 by Paul Johnson
ISBN # 978-0-9847472-0-7

Published by Safely Ever After Media

safely ever after, inc.

For information regarding permission, contact:
Safely Ever After, Inc.
1112 Montana Avenue, #277
Santa Monica, CA 90403

**www.safelyeverafter.com**

Printed in the U.S.A.

# Hi there!

My name is Katie and this is my
little brother, Kyle...
we're a lot alike.

We both like chocolate ice cream, we both like playing together outdoors. Mom says we're like 2 peas in a pod. But Kyle and I are different too. He likes to play on the swings at the park, I like the slide. He likes video games and I like to draw.

"What about you or Daddy?" Kyle asked. "Can you or Daddy look at our private parts?"

"When you and Katie were little, we helped keep your private parts clean," Mom said. "And even now, we may have to help you at bath time. That's okay."

Then Kyle asked, "What about the doctor?"

"A doctor may have to check your private parts to keep you healthy," Mom said. "It's okay if you're at the doctor' office with your Mom or Dad, but no one else should chec your private parts."

"Yeah, we don't get checkups from the ice cream man or the next-door neighbor!" I giggled. "Just the doctor."

"That's right," Mom smiled.

"What about other parts of our bodies?" I asked.

"Or other kinds of touches?" asked Kyle. "Sometimes I don't like it when Uncle Ken tickles my tummy."

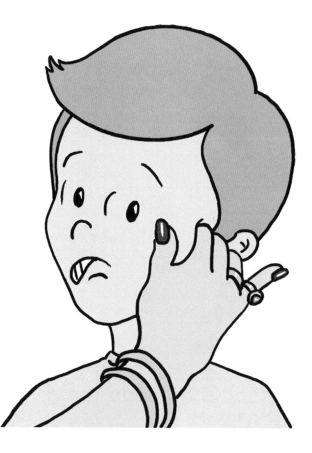

"And sometimes it makes me feel yucky when Auntie Caro[l] pinches my cheeks!"

"Those are good questions," Mom replied. "No one should touch any part of your body if you don't like it. It's okay to tell someone that you don't like their tickles or touche[s]. Even people we love, like Auntie Carol or Uncle Ken!"

"But that might hurt their feelings," said Kyle.

"Your feelings are very important too," Mom said. "And if you don't like any kind of touch, it's okay to say **stop**."

"Sometimes I like being tickled," I said.

"That's okay," said Mom. "That means tickles are fine for you. As long as no one is touching a private part, that's just fine."

"I like getting hugs, especially from Grandma," said Kyle.

"Me too!"

Mom smiled. "Most hugs and touches make us feel happy inside."

"But if you get a hug or a touch that makes you feel yucky or scared, tell that person to stop. Then come tell me or Dad about it."

Mom told us all about 'Thumbs Up' and 'Thumbs Down' touches.

A 'Thumbs Up' touch makes you feel happy, like a hug or holding your friend's hand.

A 'Thumbs Down' touch makes you feel yucky or scared.

It gives you an 'Uh-Oh' feeling.

Mom said that a 'Thumbs Down' touch is never our fault so it's important to tell our parents and never keep it a secret.

"I would never keep a secret if it gave me an ' Uh-Oh ' feeling," I said.

"Me neither!" said Kyle.  "No secrets allowed!"

Mom gave us each a hug and a kiss. "You are both very, very special, and very smart about your bodies."

"I'm going to take good care of my body," I replied.

"Me too!" shouted Kyle .

"Because my body is mine, mine, mine!"

– The End –

# Parent's Guide

safely ever after, inc.

# What Parents Can Do...

## Step 1: Understand The Reality

90% of childhood sexual abuse happens to children by someone that they know, not by a stranger. Even when it is a stranger, that person will most likely approach a child with a friendly face and an enticing trick or lure... which means your child's "stranger-danger radar" may not ever kick in. Don't expect obvious signs in a child molester or predator. These people work very hard at concealing their true nature. It is our job to be alert to the **"clues & cues"** in someone else's behavior and intentions. Child predators don't look like "the boogeyman". Most of the time, they are outgoing, super-friendly and helpful, sometimes to the point of being **almost too good to be true.** Child predators use deliberate **tricks and ploys** to gain a child's (or a parent's) trust. It's called *"grooming"*. Once they've accomplished that, they can proceed to victimize their target.

## Step 2: Reduce the Odds

Most childhood sexual abuse occurs in a secluded, one-to-one environment. Pay attention to anyone who continually insists on one-to-one access with your child which excludes you. Assess each situation/ relationship individually... *sports coach, music teacher, camp counselor, neighbor, etc.* (Not all "one-to-one" scenarios are dangerous.) Use common sense by paying attention to "red flags" to determine who should and should not be allowed to have access to your child. Show up early or unannounced on occasion if your child is alone with an adult. Pay attention to your child's mood after spending time with certain adults or older children. Do they seem withdrawn or uncomfortable? Can they clearly tell you how the time was spent or do they seem uneasy? Check several references on babysitters, camps, nannies, and others who care for children no matter how they come recommended.

## Step 3: Listen/Communicate/Educate

Begin the dialog early and often, updating the message as children grow. Use child-friendly language and non-fearful examples. Introduce the concept of *"Tricky People"*... someone who tries to "trick" a child into breaking a safety rule or engaging in "thumbs down" activities (*Tricky People* works because it covers: people you know, don't know or know just a little bit!) Let your child know they can come to you anytime they get an *"uh-oh"* feeling. If your child does tells you about someone's inappropriate actions, language or touch: Do not over-react or under-react. Let them know it's not their fault. Believe your child! Create a safe, trusting environment in which your child feels comfortable coming to you for any reason.

# Prevention Tips For Pro-Active Parents

Use the **anatomically correct terms** for private parts. Teach kids to use this language.

**Teach your child that it's OK to say** *"NO"* to anyone whose actions make them feel weird, yucky, or uncomfortable... even an adult or an older kid. They can use active phrases like: *"Stop it"*, *"I don't like that"*, *"That's not okay"* or *"You shouldn't touch me like that"*.

**Listen to your child.** If they consistently don't want to be around a particular person or environment, don't force them. They may be sensing a "red flag" that you are unaware of.

Remind kids about the important *"No Secrets"* **family rule.**

**Don't write your child's name** on the outside of their personal belongings such as a jacket or backpack.

Let children decide for themselves how they want to express affection. **Don't force them to hug or kiss another person** if they are visibly uncomfortable doing so.

**Trust your instinct** and let children know it's okay for them to trust theirs. Our instinct is one of the best barometers for letting us know when something or someone is "thumbs down".

**Practice personal safety strategies** with your kids in a non-fearful, upbeat manner. Find teachable moments... while driving to a playdate or other outing, setting the table at dinnertime, etc. You can use playful *"what if"* scenarios to help your child understand.

**Give simple, clear examples...**
  • Never get into a car or enter someone's home unless you already have your parents' permission.
  • Never take candy or any treat from someone you don't know no matter how nice they may seem.
  • Tell mom or dad about any "uh-oh" feeling or "thumbs down touch".

**Be alert** to any sudden sexual behavior or knowledge that your child exhibits which is not appropriate for their age, maturity or developmental level – especially if they have new words for their private parts. Look into reasons why and consider who may have introduced this information to them.

Be sure your child understands that if someone does make them feel "yucky" or uncomfortable, it's **never their fault** and they **won't be in trouble** for telling you. Kids will often keep a shameful secret for fear of being blamed or getting into trouble.

**Start the safety dialog** with your children early on by giving them information in small tidbits, a little bit at a time. No need to overwhelm your kids with long lectures, scare tactics, or complicated concepts.

Remember:  The **ONE thing that deters** a child predator
or a molester is the possibility that
they could get caught.

If they think YOU are paying attention and alert to their tricks…

If they think your child is confident enough to recognize thumbs down behavior, or may speak up...

YOU significantly lower the risk of being their target.

## Pattie Fitzgerald
### *Certified Child Predator Safety Educator*
*Founder, Safely Ever After, Inc.*

Pattie Fitzgerald is the founder of **Safely Ever After, Inc**. and is recognized as a leading expert in the field of childhood sexual abuse prevention education. She is certified as a Child Safety Educator and Child Visitation Monitor, and has been working in the field of child advocacy for over fifteen years. As a **former preschool teacher,** Pattie blends her expertise as an educator and, more importantly as a **MOM**, to teach parents and children every where the most effective, up-to-date safety strategies WITHOUT using fear tactics.

Admired for her positive approach, Pattie has created her unique brand of *"Safe-Smarts"*. She is a highly sought after guest lecturer and keynote speaker throughout the country, addressing the need for stronger child safety legislation and sexual abuse prevention education within our schools.

Her **Super Duper Safety Tips** and **curriculum** are used in school districts throughout southern California.

Pattie is also the author of **"Super-Duper Safety"**, a personal safety book specifically for young school children. She has been featured on Good Morning America, CNN Headline News, MSNBC, and CNBC. She currently resides in Santa Monica, California.

> *"Safely Ever After, Inc. was created because... I'm a MOM first, who simply wants my daughter to be safe and still have a childhood that is fun. Keeping our kids safe shouldn't mean being scared or worried all the time. It means being able to navigate through the myriad of statistics, research and information out there, and empowering ourselves with the best weapon around: PREVENTION EDUCATION!"*
>
> *Pattie Fitzgerald*

## safely ever after, inc.

For more information, please visit **www.safelyeverafter.com**

The remaining pages have been left intentionally blank for coloring/notes.

32050672R00015